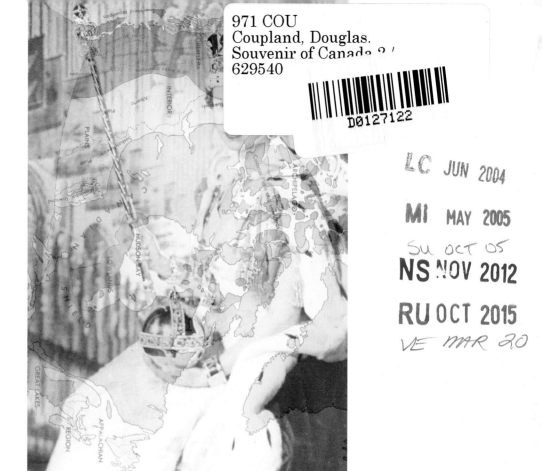

Souvenir of Canada 2
Douglas Coupland

Douglas & McIntyre
Vancouver/Toronto/Berkeley

Copyright © 2004 by Douglas Coupland

04 05 06 07 08 5 4 3 2 1

Douglas & McIntyre Ltd.
2323 Quebec Street, Suite 201
Vancouver, British Columbia
Canada V5T 4S7
www.douglas-mcintyre.com

National Library of Canada Cataloguing in Publication Data
Coupland, Douglas
Souvenir of Canada 2 / Douglas Coupland.
ISBN 1-55365-043-3
1. Canada—Social life and customs. 2. Canada—Pictorial works. I. Title.
FC90.C68 2004   971   C2004-901320-3

Library of Congress information is available upon request

Editing by Saeko Usukawa
Design by Jen Eby
Front and back cover photos by Ken Mayer Studio,
© 2002 Douglas Coupland
Front flap photo by Colwyn Griffith, *Northern Lights*
Back flap photo by Martin Tessler
Printed and bound in Canada by Friesens
Printed on acid-free paper
Distributed in the U.S. by Publishers Group West

The publisher gratefully acknowledges the financial support of the Canada Council for the Arts, the British Columbia Arts Council, and the Government of Canada through the Book Publishing Industry Development Program (BPIDP) for its publishing activities.

Every effort has been made to trace ownership of visual material used in this book. Errors or omissions will be corrected in subsequent editions, provided notification is sent to the publisher.

Title page photo: Sebastian Katz, *Canadian Shield,* giclée print

Credits

BC Hydro: 131

Roberta Bondar: 6

© Edward Burtynsky, courtesy Mira Godard Gallery: 30, 31, 96, 97

Canada Mortgage and Housing Corporation (CMHC): 16/17. From *Small House Designs*, 1965. All rights reserved. Reproduced with the consent of CMHC. All other uses and reproductions of this material are expressly prohibited.

Canadian Centennial Library: 130

© Canadian War Museum (CWM) AN19930013-509: 120/121

James Carl: 13

Dr. D.C.T. Coupland: 77

© Douglas Coupland: 110

Colwyn Griffith: 9

Health Canada: 112

Geoffrey James: 134, 135. From *Place: Lethbridge, a City on the Prairie* by Geoffrey James and Rudy Wiebe, published in Canada by Douglas & McIntyre and Southern Alberta Art Gallery, in the U.S. by David R. Godine. Reprinted by permission of the photographer.

© Brian Jennison: 14. From *Passing Trains: The Changing Face of Canadian Railroading* by Greg McDonnell, published by Boston Mills Press, reprinted with the permission of Firefly Books Ltd.

Sebastian Katz: 1

Graham Law: 142, 143, 144

Greg Locke/Stray Light Pictures: 125

© Greg McDonnell: 15, from *Wheat Kings: Vanishing Landmarks of the Canadian Prairies* and 128, 129, from *Rites of Passage: A Canadian Railway Retrospective*, both published by Boston Mills Press and reprinted with the permission of Firefly Books Ltd.

Dan Macpherson: 83

Matthew Mallon: 7

Eliza Massey: 116, 117, 118, 119

Ken Mayer Studio, © 2002 Douglas Coupland: 4, 22, 25, 72 to 75, 79, 80, 82, 89, 103, 104/105, 113, 114/115, 127

© Doug Phillips: 8. From *Passing Trains: The Changing Face of Canadian Railroading* by Greg McDonnell, published by Boston Mills Press, reprinted with the permission of Firefly Books Ltd.

Photo Technic, © 2002 Douglas Coupland: 19, 20, 21, 26, 27, 32, 33, 36, 37, 39, 70, 76, 85, 91, 92, 98, 100, 101, 121, 130, 137

Nigel Reeves: 124

Reach for the Top: 86/87

Royal Bank of Canada: 91

Boris Spremo, Toronto Star: 106/107

Ken Steacy: 108/109

Martin Tessler: 40 to 69, 103

Thanks:

Arjun Basu
Jud Beaumont
Roberta Bondar
Ed Burtynsky
Mary Jane Campbell
James Carl
Sam Carter
Anne Collins
Adam Cummins
Jen Eby
Will Ferguson
Betty and Rolly Fox
Darrell Fox
Chris Gergley
Klaus Goedecke
Elaine Gould
Colwyn Griffith
Elise Hodson

Dennis Inkster
Barb Inkster
Geoffrey James
Brian Jennison
Sebastian Katz
Atilla Kertesz Jr.
Atilla Kertesz Sr.
Brad Lamoreux
Graham Law
Greg Locke
Larry Sampson
Dan Macpherson
Greg McDonnell
Corky McIntyre
Scott McIntyre
Matthew Mallon
Eliza Massey
Ken Mayer

Malcolm Parry
Brian Paschke
Sheila Peacock
Doug Phillips
Don Prior
Nigel Reeves
Christina Ritchie
Dave Ross
Larry Sampson
Gordon & Marion Smith
Ken Steacy
Martin Tessler
Saeko Usukawa
WalMart Canada
Adele Weder
David Weir
Jean Claude Winkler
Carlyn Yandle
Sharon Young

This book ...

... rides on the coattails of the first *Souvenir* book from two years ago. As you can see, there's much that couldn't fit into that first volume. And as with the first book, themes here are arranged in a pretty much alphabetical order, with a poetic deviation here or there.

This book is dedicated to my mother. She likes to joke that she keeps the flags of all nations in the basement, but we know darn well that there's always only ever been one.

Big Country

In the summer of 1990-something, I visited London. In the car on the way into the city from Heathrow, BBC radio announced, "It's official—it's the hottest day ever in English history." The driver and I made faces at each other; I know you're supposed to discuss weather with Brits, but *this* seemed like a conversational gambit from the gods.

He asked, "Is it as hot where you come from?"

"Me? No. I'm from Vancouver. It never gets too hot or too cold there."

"Vancouver? I have a daughter there."

"Really?"

"Perhaps you know her."

Okay. This has happened to all of us. I went along with it. "Where about?"

"In Abbotsford."

Abbotsford is farming country an hour east of the city. I said, "Well, my dad keeps some cattle out there." I was happy to have a connection.

"What part of Abbotsford?"

"By the Mount Lehman highway exit."

"That's Sherry's exit. She's a block away from the Mennonite church near there."

"On Ross Road?"

"That's it."

It turns out that Sherry lives across the street from my father's cows. *Directly* across the street. The driver said, "Well, it's a small world then, isn't it?"

I said, "Yes," but in my head I was thinking, *It's more like Canada is a small country.*

Everyone thinks Canada's this vast country, but when it comes to people, no way is it huge. These days, when I'm in Europe and people ask, "Do you know So-and-so?" more often than not, I do. I've just come to expect this.

Here's a variation on this theme. In 1993, in Ireland, I learned that all of the Irish are not merely just one person away from each other—chances are they're cousins, too. It got to such an absurd point I had to mention it to somebody, who, one night, happened to be the director of a Dublin theatre. He said to me, "So you've learned Ireland's biggest secret by now then, Douglas?"

"What secret's that?"

Above: Matthew Mallon, *Rankin Inlet*, 1972

Left: Roberta Bondar, *Northern Lights*

Above: CN SD40-2 and SD40s 5184 and 5167 pilot an eastbound hotshot through the Cape Horn slide zone along the Thompson River west of Lasha, B.C., September 27, 1984.

Right: Colwyn Griffith, *Inglis Manitoba*, 2002. From the series "EyeCandy 3"

He looked around to see if anyone was listening and said, "There are only 105 people in Ireland."

This made poetic sense to me, and I tried applying the same logic to Canada, whereupon I came to the following conclusion: there are only 473 people here. And just because they're spread across thousands of kilometres, don't assume everyone's disconnected from everyone else: remember, the telephone was invented in Canada.

I guess it's all that wide open space which tricks people into thinking the country is big, but I look at it a different way—a plausible analogy to Canada might be tiny Switzerland, where, over the space of five train rides of an hour apiece, you can visit five cities with wholly different ecosystems, languages and geography. Substitute "plane" for "train," and Canada instantly becomes a small country in much the same way as Switzerland. You have Cantonese in Vancouver; prairie-twanged English in Calgary; Inuktitut up north, just about anything in Toronto, French in Quebec and, of course, Scottish in Nova Scotia.

It's always amazed me, the cavalier manner in which Canadians hop on planes and make long-distance phone calls. Space means something different to Canadians; we have a unique way of seeing ourselves. We're both a small country and a vast country. We live in six time zones, and yet everybody's just one person removed from everyone else. We are small. We are vast. The one thing we are not is merely big.

Border

In October of 2001, my Aunt Mary Jane was driving her Honda Accord from Montreal to visit friends in Maine. The Vermont border crossing was mostly empty that post-9/11 afternoon, and she was happy to sail right into the first open U.S. Customs & Immigration stall. Once she was there, the customs official at the booth said, "Good afternoon, Ma'am."

"Hello."

"Where are you off to today, then?"

"Kennebunkport—to visit friends."

"I see ..."

Pause.

He asked, "Is that your car then, Ma'am?"

"Yes, it is."

"Do you like it much?"

"Well, as a matter of fact, I do. I just got it a few months ago, and it's a real honey."

"I see. Ma'am—have you been to the doctor lately?"

Needless to say, this isn't the sort of thing you expect from a U.S. Customs agent.

"I ... well, what a strange question," my aunt said. "Funny you should ask me ... I've just come from the hospital where I had a bone scan. As a matter of fact, I've been having an awful time with arthritis, but I've been a part of a study at McGill University—some experimental shots that have worked wonders. Why do you ask?"

"Because, Ma'am, I'm looking at your car on the radioactivity scanner right now, and you're lit up like a Christmas tree. I've gotta call some of the guys in to see this. We've never seen anyone dosed up as high as you are. Carl! Randy! Come here—you've gotta see this!"

And thus, we usher in a new century of borders and permeability and trusts and alliances and relationships. Nobody comes and goes easily any more. People are no longer able to emerge from nothing.

I suppose having radioactivity monitored by machines at the U.S. border is a mixed blessing, and possibly more good than bad. Scanners searching for enriched uranium and weapons triggers also detected my aunt's arthritis. Instead of death, these scanners discovered the trail of a new chemical, one of many that reshape how we inhabit our bodies. The fact is that we truly do live in an age of miracles and wonders—there may be more darkness in the world, but there is more light, as well. I think older countries believe the opposite to be true. As a Canadian, it drives me absolutely crazy that I can't send myself a postcard from the year 3004 to see how things ended up.

Canadian Shield

We humans are picky creatures. We tend not to trust scientific evidence gleaned maybe more than a hundred years before we were born. At the same time, we are utterly unable to envision a future—any future—that exists maybe more than a hundred years beyond our individual predicted year of death. In this way, we are indeed lazy creatures. Knowing this, the Canadian Shield, to Canadians, is a lot of inescapable intellectual hard work. It's 4.5 billion years old, covers 40 per cent of the country and fully challenges our mortal notions of when time and history began, and how we fit into it. The Shield rudely and undeniably posits that time—of some sort—will continue long beyond when we humans exit this granite chip that orbits our sun.

Bleak.

Having said all of this, Canadians are proud of the Canadian Shield, our best known and oddly beloved geological formation. Yes, we have Niagara Falls, and the Americans have the Grand Canyon, but they're tourist attractions. That a country could actually boast a "Most Beloved Rock Formation" is somewhat Canadian in itself.

But let's be specific: what *is* the Canadian Shield?

It's a massive U-shaped chunk of central and eastern Canada that includes Labrador, most of Quebec, most of Ontario, most of Manitoba, half of Saskatchewan and most of Nunavut—8 million square kilometres (3 million square miles) in all. Although a portion of it dips into the U.S. Great Lakes states, it's pretty much a Canadian thing, comprising rock that bubbled forth billions of years ago. It was the first part of North America to be permanently elevated above sea level and, ever since, it has been essentially untouched by encroachments of the oceans. *Go Shield!*

Over eons, the Shield eroded to the point where the eroded bits, under the force of their own mass, compressed into the earth's crust to form sedimentary and metamorphic rocks. Yes, there will be a test.

My uncle lives in Almonte, Ontario—50 kilometres (30 miles) southwest of Ottawa, and about 13 kilometres (8 miles) southwest of Pakenham, Ontario (birthplace of basketball's inventor—an earnest Canadian fact). Growing up, I always marvelled at the way that the landscape between Pakenham and Almonte changed, with binary clarity, from dismal spruce scrub to the fertility fest that defines most of southern Ontario—all those tiny, stunted spruces and pines giving way to orchards and farms and forests. What I didn't know then is that was where the Canadian Shield ended and where the rest of the continent began. The ice-age glaciers scraped away all the soil from the Shield and deposited it on the other side. I've always hoped that Pakenham was happy to settle for basketball instead of soil.

Right: *Spring Collection*, 1990, public sculpture by James Carl, Montreal

Canola

Even as a child, I looked at the word "rapeseed" and said to myself, "Okay—*there's* a plant that needs a fresh new marketing image." Decades later, I walk down aisle five at Loblaws, and what do I see? "Canola—wonder oil of the universe"—hybridized and fresh, a great leap beyond its pungently and depressingly named predecessor. Yes, canola, formerly rapeseed, is named after Canada. And it's only when you look at something like this that you begin to realize how difficult it can be to try to cobble together a national identity from things like canola and, say, the discovery of insulin or basketball. But we're used to doing it. It keeps us humble and it keeps us trying harder at just about everything.

Left: Ex-CP FP7 1423, F9B 6652 and FP7 1418 piloting VIA No. 1, The Canadian, through the Kicking horse Pass west of Palliser, B.C., February 11, 1982.

Above: CP La Riviere Sub Wayfreight, west of Rosenfeld, Manitoba, August 1984.

CMHC Houses

As the majority of Canadians live not that far from the U.S. border, most are familiar with that weird sense of being someplace totally different that happens the *moment* you cross that invisible line. It's not just the enormous portions of food served there, nor is it the omnipresent flags and non-metric signage. There's something else at play, and three years ago I finally figured it out—it's their *houses*. Ours are different, and different for a single surprising reason: millions and millions of practically free blueprints, courtesy of CMHC (Canada Housing & Mortgage Corporation). In the decades following WWII, hundreds of house designs were made available for about fifteen dollars to Canadian homeowners and builders.

The idea was so unilaterally successful that CMHC houses brand every community in the country. In many places, they are nearly all the single-family dwellings. The designs of these houses were based on a sort of Scandinavian idea that Canadians should have good housing at affordable prices. The architecture also took into account the vast range of climates and terrains across the country, and was flexible to allow for most budgets. CMHC now publishes plans for updating these older homes, and the cycle continues.

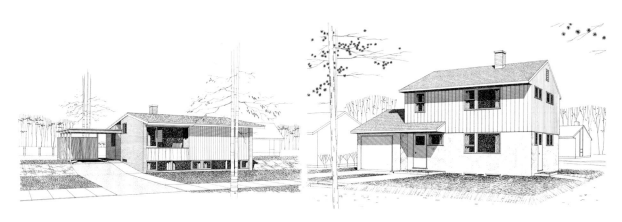

Belleville   **Truro**

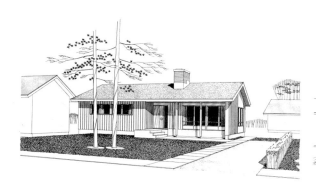

North Bay

Dollard des Ormeaux

Charlottetown

Lloydminster

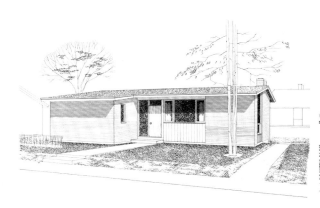

Kamloops

Brandon

Eaton's

In 1988 and into 1989, I worked in Toronto, in an office across the street from the Davisville subway stop. When the weather was pleasant, I'd ride my ten-speed into Mount Pleasant Cemetery, which was adjacent to my office building. In a big city, a cemetery remains the true bastion of silence. Forget parks or lakesides. Give me beautifully topiaried trees and warm grass amid looping, unlined paved roads. Mount Pleasant was a daily trip to a version of heaven. Added bonus: not having to deal with the living.

It sounds morbid, but one of my favourite places to eat lunch was beside the crypt of the Eaton family. Across many generations, the Eatons made, maintained and ultimately dropped the football that was Canada's most beloved department store. Why eat by their crypt? Possibly out of gratitude. For decades, Eaton's put out great catalogues, and everybody remembers Christmastime, going through those catalogues, looking for the perfect CCM bike or Spirograph kit or pair of skates.

To look at, say, a 1975 Eaton's catalogue now, is a bit jolting—all those models, seemingly selected at random from the White Pages, as well as all those scary clothes and haircuts. But on another level, you have to marvel at the sheer *inventory* a company like Eaton's would have had to maintain—not just everything shown in the catalogue, but in all colours and sizes, too— a shirt to fit your baby sister as well as Helen-with-a-goitre from the Legion. I have this picture in my head of the Eaton's warehouse, somewhere in Ontario, a building bigger than a hundred hockey rinks stacked up on top of each other, imploding from the combined weight of its inventory and a light dusting of rooftop snow. A fanciful vision, and one that could only be had by someone who once felt invincible, forever young, and who ate lunch in graveyards.

Christmas 1975

EATON'S

Index, Pricing Policy, Account, Shopping and General Information, pages 233-234.

Prices in effect until January 17, 1976 Toy prices in effect until February 28, 1976.

Where to find our cover fashions: Gown sold on page 3. Men's suit page 433, shirt and tie page 407. Girls' dress page 100. Boys' outfit page 91.

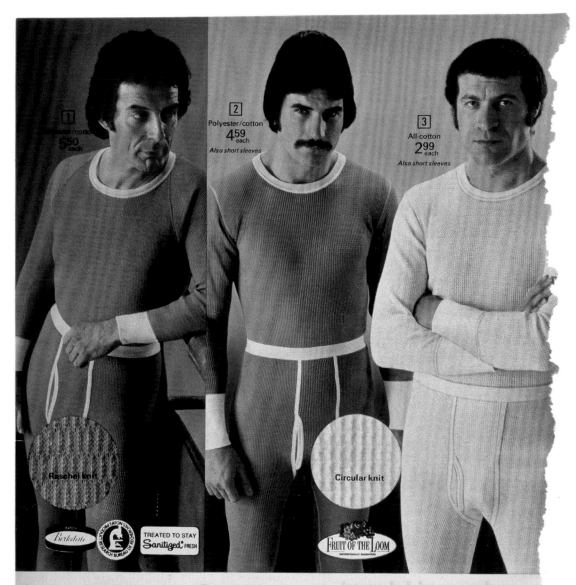

1 Polyester/cotton **5.50** each

2 Polyester/cotton **4.59** each
Also short sleeves

3 All-cotton **2.99** each
Also short sleeves

Raschel knit

Circular knit

Birkdale · EATON STOCKROOM RESEARCH BUREAU OF · TREATED TO STAY *Sanitized* FRESH

FRUIT OF THE LOOM UNCONDITIONALLY GUARANTEED

Thermals keep you dry

1 Eaton Birkdale—our very best in thermal comfort! Best because raschel knit waffle-cloth keeps you warmer and drier; thanks to extra-deep air cells that seal in more body heat than circular knits. Best because our blend of polyester/cotton combines absorbent comfort with long wear and great shape retention. Best because they're *Sanitized* to resist perspiration odours; stay fresh and new longer. And best because Birkdale thermals are tough-tested and approved by Eaton's Research Bureau! Machine wash and dry.
Colours: 41-medium blue; 70-white.
†Men's sizes: S, M, L, XL.
Shirts: crew neck; no-bind raglan sleeves.
25-H 9834B—Long sleeves. Each 5.50
25-H 9831B—Short sleeves. Each 5.50
Drawers: elastic waist; double-ply crotch.
25-H 9833B—Ankle-length. Each 5.50

2 and **3** Fruit of the Loom thermals, in two economical qualities. Both feature circular-type knit for good thermal absorbency and flatlock seams for a smooth, comfortable fit. Buy in two's for better value!
†Men's sizes: S, M, L, XL.

(2) Better quality: polyester blended with cotton for long wear and soft comfort. Machine wash and dry at low temperatures.
Colours: order by number and name.
41-medium blue; 70-white.
Shirts: crew-neck pullover style.
25-H 9434BS—Long sleeves. Each 4.59
25-H 9431B—Short sleeves 3.99; 2/7.90
Drawers: elastic waist; taped front seams.
25-H 9433BS—Ankle-length. Each 4.59
  Long-sleeve shirt and drawers—any 2 for 9.00

(3) Good quality: all-cotton for absorbent comfort. White only; machine wash, lay flat to dry.
Shirts: crew-neck pullover style.
25-H 9444AS—Long sleeves. Each 2.99
25-H 9441A—Short sleeves 2.79; 2/5.50
Drawers: elastic waist; taped front seams.
25-H 9443AS—Ankle length. Each 2.99
  Long-sleeve shirt and drawers—any 2 for 5.90

†Men's underwear size chart.

Size	S	M	L	XL
Chest	34-36	38-40	42-44	46
Waist	30-32	34-36	38-40	42-44

How-to-measure, page 395.

There is a small order handling charge of 50¢ on orders totalling under $5.00. See page 888.

1 2 3 4

N Shirt 4⁵⁰
Longjohns 4⁵⁰

O Shirt 5⁰⁰
Longjohns 5⁰⁰

R Shirt 7⁰⁰
Longjohns 7⁰⁰

Shirt 6⁵⁰
Longjohns 6⁵⁰

Super selection of lightweight warmers!

N Fruit of the Loom shirt and long-johns in pretty blue floral print on white. Thermal knit cotton underwear is specially designed with thousands of tiny air pockets to trap body heat and keep out the cold. Easy care too, just machine wash.

The shirt: neat rib knit at neckline and cuffs of long sleeves.
Busts: S(32-34), M(36-38), L(40-42).
9-H 6684AS—Each 4.50
Any 2 for 8.90

Longjohns: rib knit at cuffs; wide elastic at the waist.
Hips: S(37-39), M(40-43), L(44-47).
9-H 6685AS—Each 4.50
Any 2 for 8.90

O Cosy underwear, expertly made by Stanfield's. In a warm blend of cotton, for absorbency and comfort and polyester for strength and longer life. Knit fabric provides added insulation. Machine washable.
Colours: 01-pink; 41-blue.

The shirt: rib knit at neck; Lycra (spandex) in cuffs, for snug fit.
Busts: S(34-36), M(38-40), L(42-44).
9-H 6688BS—Each 5.00
Any 2 for 9.90

Longjohns: Lycra (spandex) in cuffs; wide elastic at the waist.
Hips: S(34-36), M(38-40), L(42-44).
9-H 6689BS—Each 5.00
Any 2 for 9.90

P Toasty warm underwear. In a smart blend of polyester for strength and durability, and cotton, for comfort and absorbency. Interlock construction provides added insulation. Resists runs from snags. Screen print design on shirt front. Machine wash. Light blue/white.

The shirt: double rib knit at neck and cuffs for more comfort, neater fit.
Busts: S(34-36), M(38-40), L(42-44).
9-H 6699A—Each 6.50

Longjohns: rib knit cuffs; white elastic waist, cotton-covered for wear.
Hips: S(34-36), M(38-40), L(42-44).
9-H 6700A—Each 6.50

R Ski underwear that looks great for après ski lounging. In a blend of polyester for strength, and cotton for absorbency. Interlock fabric means more warmth; it doesn't run easily if snagged; has good recovery. Machine wash. Red with black/white.

The shirt: double rib knit neck, cuffs, for added comfort and strength.
Busts: S(34-36), M(38-40), L(42-44).
9-H 6690A—Each 7.00

Longjohns: cotton-covered black elastic waist; black/white contrast.
Hips: S(34-36), M(38-40), L(42-44).
9-H 6691A—Each 7.00

SAVE 10% on shirt/longjohns set.
9-H 6661AE—Set 12.58

All four versatile styles above may be used as underwear, for lounging and for sleepwear.

1 2 3 4

Energy

gasoline

birch log

eggs

diesel oil

aviation fuel

rum

transmission fuel

charcoal

outboard motor oil

butane

manure

baked beans

lard

wind-up flashlight

candles

canola

propane

butter

fuel log

doughnut

apple

battery

whisky

ham

condensed milk

water (glass half empty/full)

flour

beer

wine

potato

insulation

transmission fluid

peanut butter

uranium

motor oil

Fish

Fish, more than any other wildlife, give us a potent, undeniable health report on our land and our culture. Symbolically, fish are our soul, and to be a fish in Canada right now is a very depressing thing. If you're an overfished Atlantic cod off Newfoundland's Grand Banks, it means you'll probably never grow to your 200-centimetre (6.5-foot) potential and that your position in the food web (or chain, depending on your philosophy) is permanently imperilled— to a point where many experts think that you'll soon be extinct.

On the Pacific, if you're a farmed Atlantic salmon, you're bred in cages up the coast, and the colour of your flesh will be determined by the amount of synthetic astaxanthin you're fed— a chemical that can regulate your flesh tone from beige to sunburnt. Pacific salmon, luckily, are too oily, their flesh too colourful, for this sort of modification—hence the use of Atlantic salmon. Also, as a farmed fish on the west coast, you'll be fed antibiotics, which create microbial havoc with indigenous species. And the flesh of nearby oysters and clams, which have been sucking up all that stray astaxanthin, will also turn red.

Freshwater fish don't fare much better. Sturgeon in the Fraser River are vanishing, and nobody knows why, but everyone can pretty much guess, and everyone's guess is probably accurate. As well, inland trout that receive airborne toxins from Asia are becoming hermaphroditic and unable to reproduce. Lead shot in prairie lakes is poisoning the few fish that survive to spawn. In the Great Lakes, any number of new and invasive species are on the brink of pushing out the indigenous stocks, with a splash of acid rain thrown in.

We are appalling stewards of our country's waters. We worry that the Americans are planning to steal it, but when the time comes, will they even want it? We are greedy and stupid and lazy. We'll happily trade fifty jobs for the extinction of an entire species. The key word here is JOBS. It's the word that people hurl in your face whenever you discuss changing fishing or lumber practices.

I think that governments like to camouflage the real problem by conning people into an irrelevant jobs/extinction argument. The real problem is that we ship not only our fish but also our logs and ore overseas where it's the JOB of non-Canadians to add value to them and then sell them back to us. Remember: Canada, well into the twentieth century, was both a plaything and a magical resource-making machine for England. We often think like serfs and expect to be treated as such. We're smarter than this, and if we don't start adding brains to our resources, it'll probably be the end of us.

Right: Whale embryo

26

23P66
HAFL

CANUCK

Calibre 12, 2¾ Pouces
Cartouches Fortes
Choix de Charges
2, 4, 5, 6, 7½, BB

RECOMMANDÉES

Renard	BB
Lièvre de Prairies	2, 4 ou BB
Oie	2 ou BB
Canard, Lièvre	4, 5 ou 6
Oiseaux non-aquatiques	6 ou 7½
Bécassine, Bécasse	7½

IMPORTANT

N'employez que dans les fusils construits pour tirer des cartouches à poudre sans fumée. Ne les tirez pas avec des fusils ayant une chambre plus courte que 2¾ pouces.

N'exposez pas à la chaleur — Gardez dans un endroit sec et frais.

CANUCK
HEAVY LOAD

PLASTIC SHELL

WARNING	C·I·L	12 GAUGE
KEEP OUT OF REACH OF CHILDREN		2¾ INCH

57973

CANUCK
HEAVY

12 GAUGE **C·I·L**
2¾ INCH

25 SHOT
SHELLS

MANUFACTURED BY
CANADIAN INDUSTRIES LIMITED
MONTREAL, CANADA

SGP-121

Guns & Ammo

I grew up around guns and have no problem with them. I think that's true of most Canadians who've grown up around guns and ammo. When I was young, my father used to go to skeet shoots; my brothers and I would be brought along with the dog. As there was nothing else to do, we'd go out onto the range and collect the stray clay pigeons that didn't get shot or shatter on landing. Our plan was always to open up a lemonade stand that sold both lemonade and clay pigeons as ashtrays. So, we'd be out there combing the grass while shots flew about 15 metres (50 feet) above our heads. Our one instruction? *Don't get hit.*

I was also taken along on hunting trips, and as both my father and brother are champion marksmen, we always arrived home laden with blood, feathers, grouse and pheasant. My brother is also an expert taxidermist (birds only). If a trumpeter swan ever snags its neck and strangles itself on power lines over your property, he's the guy to call.

Question: Do we have a gun problem? No.

Question: Do we have a government problem? Well, sort of—the Canadian government has a registration plan that has been botched and is loathed by most everybody, but give my dad a drink and he'll fill you in on that.

Halifax

In 1988, I worked in the fact-checking department of a Toronto business magazine. That was the year that faxes became cool and groovy, and when you told someone you had a fax machine, they'd make the ooohhh noise. I remember Susan from ad sales coming into the editorial area, saying, "Faxes are hot! Can't you people do something interesting with fax machines?"

I thus came up with "Celebrity Fax of the Month." Pure froth, but fun, too—a supermodel faxed us a lipstick kiss from the Hotel George Cinq in Paris, and a hockey player from the Soviet Union faxed us a photocopy of a hockey puck from the Canadian Embassy in Moscow. After a short while, though, we were becoming desperate for fax ideas, and so, as a last gasp, I phoned the mayor of Halifax, Ron Wallace, and asked him if he would fax us a letter stating, "As Mayor of Halifax, I am proud that the name of my city contains the word 'fax,' the hottest and most exciting mode of business communication in the world." And he did. Back in 1988, you could do that—simply pick up the phone and call the mayor of Halifax. Nowadays, you have to pass through a screen of sceptical media handlers, a three-tiered security clearance, a retinal scan, plus a computerized background inspection form that must be submitted five working days in advance. It was another era.

Five Halifax fun facts:
1) People from the city are called Haligonians (only Canadians ever know that).
2) It has the world's second-largest natural harbour.
3) Bodies recovered from the *Titanic* are buried in Halifax.
4) In that game of "Geography"—the game you play when you're driving on long trips, the one where you name a place and the next person has to name a place that begins with the last letter of that name—Halifax is the city that always ends the game.
5) My grandfather had a Nova Scotia–related joke we never tired of. He'd ask us if we wanted a picture of the *Bluenose*, a sailing ship from Lunenburg, Nova Scotia. We'd say yes, and he'd say it'll cost a quarter, and so we'd give him a quarter, and he'd give us a dime on which the *Bluenose* appeared. It was on the dime from 1937 up until 2000.

Edward Burtynsky, *Polyfoam Resurrections, Showroom and Office* Hanover, Ontario, 1982

Edward Burtynsky, *Polyfoam Resurrections, Workbench,* Hundred Mile House, B.C., 1983

THE BLUENOSE

Champion Racing Schooner of the Grand Banks

Schooner de compétion champion des Grands Bancs

Scale 1:120   Échelle 1/120

HOBBY CRAFT

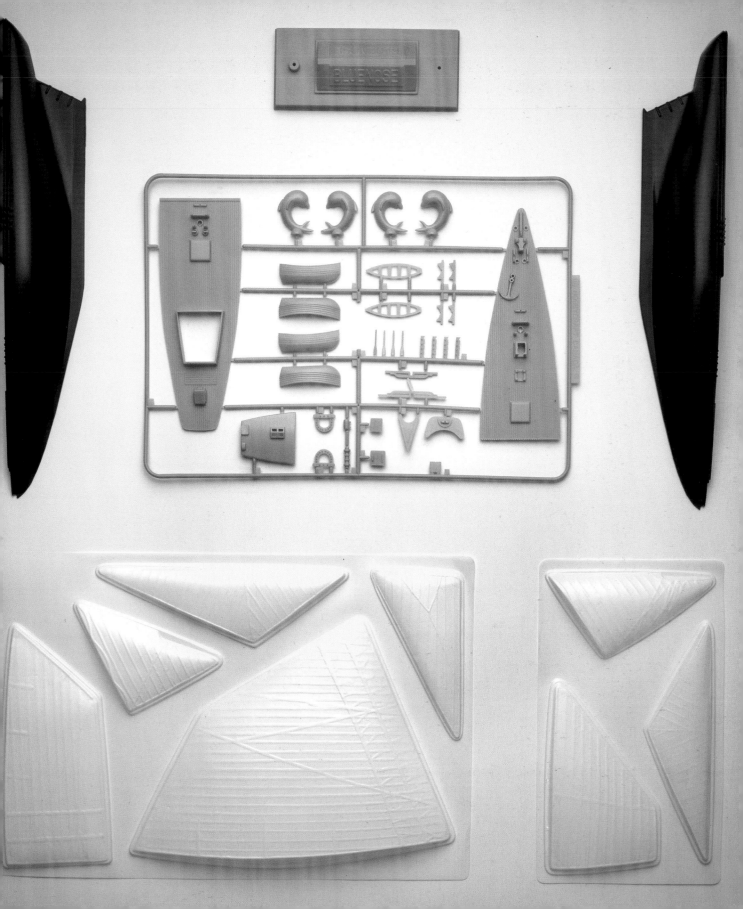

Gitchigumi

EDMUND FITZGERALD

US.277437, Lake Bulk Freighter built in 1958,

Great Lakes Engineering Works, River Rouge, MI, Hull No. 301.

Crew list, November 10, 1975

Captain Ernest M. McSorley
Michael E. Armagost
Fred J. Beetcher
Thomas D. Bentsen
Edward F. Bindonz
Thomas D. Borgeson
Oliver J. Champeau
Nolan S. Church

Ransom E. Cundy
Thomas E. Edwards
Russell G. Haskell
George J. Holl
Bruce L. Hudson
Allen G. Kalmon
John H. McCarthy
Gorden F. MacLellan

Joseph W. Mazes
Eugene W. O'Brien
Karl A. Peckol
John J. Poviach
James A. Pratt
Robert C. Rafferty
Paul M. Riippa
John D. Simmons

William J. Spengler
Mark A. Thomas
Ralph G. Walton
David E. Weiss
Blaine H. Wilhelm

GST

The single most hated thing in all of Canada is the GST—the Goods and Services Tax—a 7 per cent ~~money grab~~ tax on almost all but a tiny few facets of Canadian life. The GST was introduced in 1991 as a temporary means of combatting the national debt and of "harmonizing" previously existing complex tax structures. Yeah, right.

As with any tax, once it's introduced, it never goes away. In a few provinces, the GST has been merged with the provincial tax, but in the end, it's one great big money suck, and we're saddled with it forever. Here we are, a dozen years later, still wondering how we were stupid enough to let this happen. In some sick, backhanded way, the fact that we did so proves that we deserve it.

Hardware

This is really weird—brace yourself: there's a special kind of screw and screwdriver used almost exclusively in Canada—not even in England or Australia. It's called a Robertson, but only Canadians know that.

Once, in Manhattan, I was in a hotel lobby while a UPS guy by the concierge desk was trying to open a crate sent from Canada. He was having no success, so I looked at the screw heads, and they were Robertsons, so I said, "Those are Robertson screws. You'll need a Robertson screwdriver for that."

"No we won't." The concierge went into the room out back, brought out a crowbar and said, "Here in New York we call those things *crowbar* screws." He then jimmied open the crate.

In subsequent years, when work took me to art gallery and museum loading docks and shipping departments, I asked them all what they do when they get a Robertson screw. They always pointed to the crowbar. So now, as a gift for people in the art world, I always bring a Canadian Tire Robertson screwdriver.

Hooch

Younger people are shocked to learn that between 1920 and 1933, alcohol was illegal in the United States. During those prohibition years, Canada, a generally abstemious nation, became the back-door bartender to its thirsty and bored southern neighbour. Along the way, some great fortunes were made, and Canada became a pretty good maker of whisky and beer.

Lest Canada's citizens become too enamoured of alcohol, the country's provincial governments began a battle that is only recently coming to an end—a battle with each other as to which province has the bleakest liquor stores, the most joyless staff and the most irksome sales procedure. In Ontario in the 1960s, you had to fill out a form at one window and then take the form over to another window, where finally a staff member went (with pursed lips, I imagine) to pick up your hooch. Those days are gone, but nowadays, thanks to heavy alcohol taxation, a similar moral tone prevails.

Canada House

What Is Canada House?

For years, I've been collecting images, objects, scraps and ideas with the end purpose of using them to build a uniquely Canadian environment. What you see on the previous two and the following twenty-seven pages is the result of that project. In November of 2003, I was given two weeks to do whatever I wanted to a sprawling, 1950s flat-roofed clunker of a house in Vancouver—a house built along the same principles of the CMHC houses that appear as a category in this book. The house had lain unheated and unused for two years, and was slated for demolition—ivy was growing in the windows and the walls were scrawled with graffiti. Some of its fixtures had been removed, and contractors had punctured holes in the wall to inspect the drywall for removal.

The first thing I did was to wrap the outsides with black plastic. After this, the walls, floors, windows, sinks, ovens and everything else were sprayed with three coats of white latex paint, giving the inside a ghostly, futuristic feel. Because the house was slated for wrecking, it was technically as much a piece of scrap as any of the driftwood, castoffs and leftovers I'd gathered over the years. Working in the house was strange, because if I had litter, all I had to do was to open a cupboard and toss it in. If I needed to make a diagram to explain something, I just wrote it on the walls. It felt outrageously liberating, a bit like architectural skinny-dipping.

Canada House was really only "open" for about five days. Record rainfalls created spontaneous lakes in the middle of some of the rooms. The heating, iffy at its best, died after day two. The floors got dirty very quickly, so visitors politely wore elasticized blue plastic surgery booties.

The objects I made for the insides work as both art and design, and they come in two categories. The first is quilts and cabinets and the like, which are made from scraps.

The second is objects, in which I took an idea, and then turned it into a concrete object. For example, I made two streamlined sofas, one called "Two Solitudes" (a Victorian kissing chair upholstered with red and blue "hoser" fabric), and another called the "Treaty Sofa." Both express notions of Canadian society, and both are shown on pages 43 and 44.

Upon entering the house, the first thing a visitor saw was the front stairwell area. It was filled with a strand of fishing floats and boat fenders, numbered in accordance with superstitious rules that I saw in an elevator in a friend's building in Vancouver. The number 13 is absent, as are numbers containing 4 or 7, which are both considered unlucky in Chinese culture. Thus, a twelve-storey building looks like it has sixteen storeys: 1, 2, 3, 5, 6, 8, 9, 10, 11, 12, 15 and 16!

Throughout the house, there was also a variety of quilts and blankets. The quilts were made from just about everything you can find on a Canadian road or in a Canadian house— for starters, municipal recycling bags, cheesy animal T-shirts, NHL-logo drapes and paper potato sacks. The "$1,000 Blanket," a few pages ahead, is adorned with one thousand loonies; it's a play on the west coast Native peoples' button blanket, and when you put it on, it feels like you're wearing a dental X-ray radiation shield. The "Hubcap Quilt" has hubcaps from Canadian Tire and is perforated with catgut dream catchers. Both pieces were included in Kitchener's Grand National Quilt Exhibition of 2004 (… he said, giving himself and his seamstresses Sharon and Carlyn a pat on the back).

Also placed throughout the house were standing lamps made from stacked fishing floats. Most of the floats were gathered in August of 2003, on a trip I made up the coast of Graham Island in northern Haida Gwaii (the Queen Charlotte Islands). Along for the trip was a good friend, Canadian painter Gordon Smith. After finding more than a hundred floats, as well as countless Japanese and Korean shampoo bottles and whiskey bottles, I began to look at this debris from two viewpoints: 1) *Wow! All of these beautiful treasure-like things just lying here, free!* and 2) *Holy crap! All of this plastic junk littering these otherwise pristine beaches!* At the dock in Queen Charlotte City, a trio of hippies (yes, hippies) said, "Whoa! Going out and cleaning up Mother Nature on your own time—awesome, dudes!" I nodded sagely.

Speaking of Gordon, when I was in his studio in 2002, I looked into his acrylic paint pots, and what I saw was so beautiful that I took a dozen pots and photographed them, creating the planet-like shapes you see in the frames—a Rorschach test peek into the Canadian painter's soul. And those goose decoys? Read the final essay in this book, and you'll find out how much a part of my life geese have been and continue to be.

Canada is a northern country, and because of this, plastics can take tens of thousands of times longer to decompose than they might at the Equator with all its heat, sunlight and bacteria. Plastics discarded in the far Arctic will remain intact until, scientifically, mathematically, our universe ends. The chunks of foam you see on page 51 were found on the tidal flats beneath Vancouver's Lions Gate Bridge. Here, they form an *inuksuk* (plural: *inuksuit*), a communication and art form originated by the Inuit in Canada's far north. Inuksuit are made of rocks that are piled into various types of shapes. They've existed in the north for several thousand years, and have only recently entered public awareness south of the Arctic Circle.

The above photo shows a pile of mussel shells on the floor of what was once a bathroom. These shells remind me of my family's brief stop in Halifax and of Montreal restaurants, back in 1988 when I was broke, getting older and had no idea what life would bring: *Moules Marinière.*

One of the great things about photographing the rooms in Canada House was that if a wall was in the way, we simply got out the chainsaw and removed it, hence the above shot of float lamps.

On the following pages is what I called the "Hoser Room"—a room inhabited by the amusing and harmless mythical Canadian hoser.

A hoser is a beer-drinking, *eh*-saying gallunk who lives in his parents' basement and watches cable TV while wearing a combination of hockey garb, hunting gear and army surplus accessories. He's probably a night manager at the local PetroCan and genuinely loves the cold and dark of winter. He's full of both goodwill and hockey statistics, and even if he's married, he somehow manages to continue living in his parents' basement.

The quilt on the floor was made using a pattern from an old *Chatelaine*, a Canadian women's magazine. The pattern features Canada's official 1967 Centennial logo. The quilt is slightly sweet and sad and ancient, and visitors younger than thirty asked, *What's that maple leaf logo thingy?*

In the mid-1980s, I had a job designing baby cribs (I know, random) in one of the few factories around Vancouver that actually made anything useful out of B.C.'s wood. It was a wonderful job that taught me a hundred incidental skills beyond simply designing an object. So, in the 1990s, when an Alberta furniture company asked me to design stuff for them, I was happy to revisit my roots. What evolved was a series of simple tables that explored Canadian themes. The most popular was (and continues to be) "Hockey Night in Canada," which is also a nod to curling rinks and the RCAF emblem. Others were "Haida," "Expo '67" and "Jasper" (Alberta). On the wall shown here are experiments and leftovers from that project.

After this photo, there are a variety of pieces. The antler chair was made in 1994, but it was so perfect and shiny that it looked fake, so I put it near the creek, where it aged in dignity until the squirrels discovered in around 1998. Hungry for sodium, they gnawed away at it, filing the antler tips sharp enough to make even a seasoned junkie cringe. Algae gave it that finishing touch.

As for the blanket, it's a loving tribute to the dot paintings of English artist Damien Hirst—an updated way of showcasing a widespread tendency of Canadians to be Anglophiles, a tendency both endearing and crippling. A friend once asked me what I thought of the monarchy in Canada. I said I didn't mind it. There's no real reason to get rid of it, and, to a point, it does make us who we are. But I'd also demand online referendums be held as to whether or not photos of monarchs appear on money and stamps, and if so, which images. Our paper money is homely enough already.

The two tables on pages 62 and 63 were built to accompany the two sofas pictured earlier. One is called "Talking in Circles," and the other is called "Never Ending Story." Both are wood sheets inlaid with scale model–railway track. When thinking of Canadian history, you can never underestimate the power of the railway. If it hadn't been built, the U.S. would be about fifty-eight to sixty states right now instead of fifty. The railway made Canada, Canada.

The snow tire was found, inexplicably, in the cupboard just to the left of the shot, and was so serendipitous that we included it. The snow tire reminds me of an article I once read about traffic deaths in Ontario in winter. It turns out that the people who die the most in vehicles in winter are the ones who drive to the corner store for smokes in minus-20 weather, wearing only a T-shirt. The engine dies or the gas runs out, and before you know it, it's curtains. This may be an urban legend, but I doubt it. The cold is evil. It lies in wait for you.

The quilt on the wall is made of thick unbleached cotton perforated with dream catchers, no hubcaps this time. My friend Carlyn, who was the seamstress on the "Hubcap Quilt," wanted to make something pretty after her long ordeal working on it—this was her reward. It's called the "Pretty Dream Catcher" quilt. To be honest, it should have been photographed against a dark background. Sorry, Carlyn—but yes, it is *very* pretty.

The fireplace is a 1950s stone fireplace. Before it was painted it looked okay, but once it was painted white?—it rocked! And everyone agreed it was extremely Canadian in a way that was hard to define. That's a good thing.

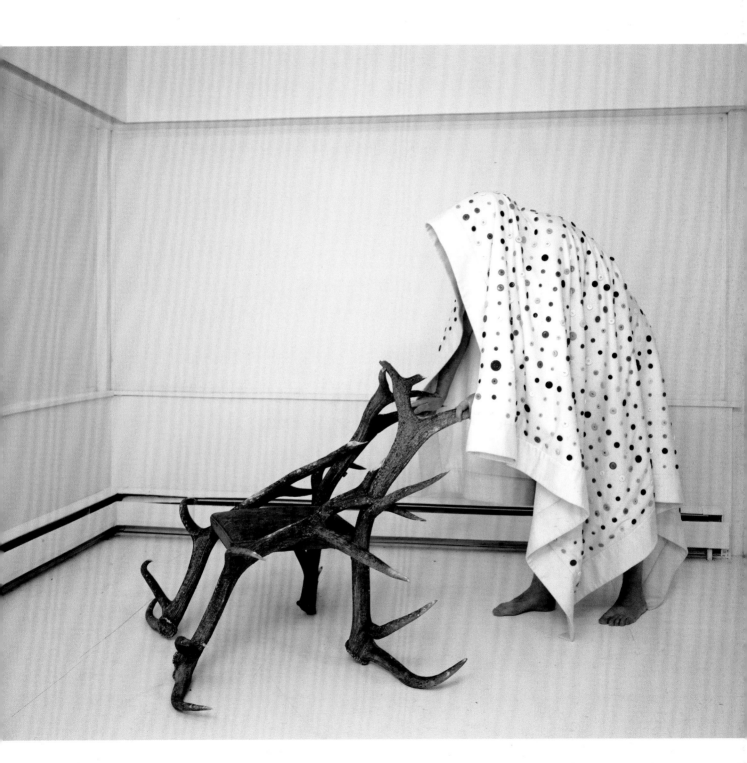

The photo to the left shows details of textile pieces in Canada House. In the pages following this are shots from the basement and kitchen.

In the basement, there was a series of four high-tension line towers made from the same birch plywood used for hockey sticks. In B.C.'s Fraser Valley, lines carrying power all the way from the Peace River run beside my father's cattle land. Not that there's a correlation or anything, BUT I've seen just about everything that can go wrong with bovine midwifery—two-headed calves? Sure. Extra legs? Yup. *Looks like trouble—bring the truck over and start the winch.* Power lines: good or evil?
I have no idea why I'm not a vegetarian.

The kitchen, of all the rooms, was the most startling when painted all white—the stove being the most potent white item. The blue globe in the background was made of forty-two water bottles from a bottling company that friends of mine started and for which I did design work nearly two decades ago. For obvious reasons, I called it "The Water Planet." The ladder, I called "The Spawning Ladder." The colours came from a scientific measuring system that allows fish farmers to pre-select the flesh tone of their fish—ugh.

Before we leave Canada House, one final anecdote …

On the Saturday night when the house was up and running, I had a small get-together for friends who helped to prepare the house. I didn't want to make the white surfaces any muckier than I had to, so I decided to serve only B.C. white wine in stylishly affordable styrofoam cups. In order for everyone to be able to tell whose cup was whose, I asked people to write their name and hometown on their cup. I thought people might interpret this as control freakdom, but instead, everybody clung onto their cups like they were baby puppies. My guests compared their cups with everybody else's, and it was odd, because people you thought you knew really well came from hometowns they'd never mentioned before: Flin Flon, Antigonish, Whitehorse … I saved them all, and every province and territory was represented there that night. It's a small fact, but it's one that made me proud.

BLUE
RIBBON

PURE
GINGER
1¼ OZ. NET

1½ OZS.   NET WEIGHT

TUXEDO

PURE

CAYENNE PEPPER

Woodward's SUPREME
BRAND
BLACK
PEPPERCORNS
NET WEIGHT 1 3/4 OZ.

for WOODWARD STORES LIMITED, Vanc...

EMPRESS

PURE
MARJORAM
1 OZ. NET WT.

S

SCHWARTZ

PURE
THYME
THYM
3/4 OZ. NET WT.

EMPRESS

PURE

CINNAMON
4 OZ. NET WT.

PURE
POULTRY
SEASONING
NABOB

PURE
MARJORAM
1 oz. net
MARJOLAINE
Blue Ribbon

Kitchen

About a year ago, on a Tuesday morning at 11:30 a.m., I phoned my mother and said, "Mom, I'm going to be there in a half-hour with a photographer to document your kitchen. Don't touch anything." It says much about my family that my mother shrugged, thought to herself, *Well, he* does *manage to feed himself by doing all this crazy stuff,* and left the kitchen unsullied.

I asked her not to touch anything because I wanted the photographer to capture the truth—and the truth is that my mother's kitchen shelves could easily win a Most Canadian Shelves award. The photos presented here speak for themselves. You can't see it in the photos, but a grilled cheese sandwich and cauliflower soup are being cooked on the other side of the room. If your mother's kitchen isn't nearby, please allow my own mother's cupboards to warm your soul.

Note: A few years ago, my mother went through a vinegar phase, so for Christmas I bought her a vinegars-of-the-world collection. Now she collects really good knives, which is slightly scary.

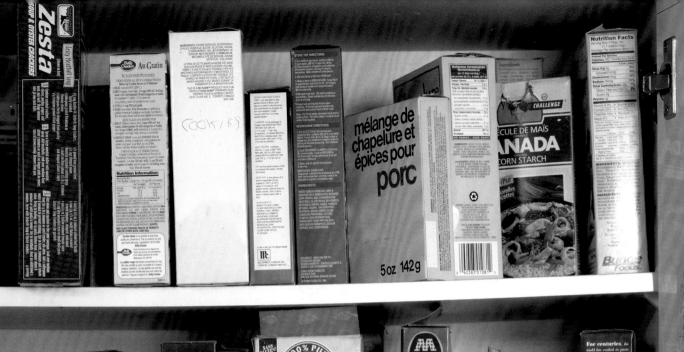

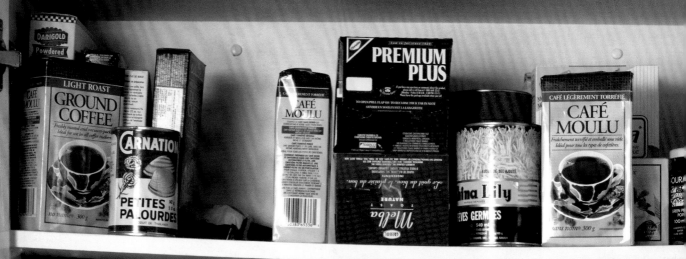

Robin Hood

Original

Nanaimo Bar MIX

760 g

NO BAKE TREAT

Original

Nanaimo Bar MIX

PREPARATION DIRECTIONS:
GREASE one 9" (20 cm) square pan.

BASE:
COMBINE in mixing bowl:
• Base Mix (Pouch A)
• 1/2 cup (125 mL) butter or margarine, melted
MIX well. Mixture will be wet.
PRESS firmly in prepared pan.
CHILL while preparing filling.

FILLING:
COMBINE in small mixer bowl:
• Filling Mix (Pouch B)
• 2 tbsp (30 mL) butter or margarine, softened
• 2 tbsp (30 mL) hot water
BEAT at low speed of electric mixer until blend, then at high speed until smooth and creamy, about 2 minutes.
SPREAD evenly over base.
CHILL until firm, about 30 minutes.

TOPPING:
COMBINE in small saucepan or microwave-safe bowl:
• Topping Mix (Pouch C)
• 3 tbsp (45 mL) butter or margarine
HEAT at low or in microwave at medium, stirring until smooth, melted.
SPREAD quickly and evenly over filling.
CHILL until chocolate is set, about 15 minutes.
CUT into bars.
STORE in refrigerator.
MAKES 24 (1" x 1-1/2" or 2.5 x 3.5 cm) bars.

INGREDIENT LISTING: ICING SUGAR, RICE SUGAR, ROBIN HOOD FLOUR, CHOCOLATE CHIPS (SUGAR, CHOCOLATE LIQUOR, COCOA BUTTER, LECITHIN, ARTIFICIAL FLAVOUR), VEGETABLE OIL SHORTENING, COCOA, CHOPPED WALNUTS, PROPYLENE GLYCOL MONO FATTY ACID ESTERS, CORN SYRUP SOLIDS, COCONUT, MAY CONTAIN SULPHITES, ARTIFICIAL FLAVOUR, DRY SOUR MILK, SALT, MODIFIED CORN STARCH, BAKING SODA, LECITHIN, CALCIUM CARRAGEENAN, COLOUR, TRI-ETHYL CITRATE, DIBASIC SODIUM PHOSPHATE, POLYSORBATE 80, MAY CONTAIN NATURAL FLAVOUR.

robin hood
multifoods
inc.
60 COLUMBIA WAY
MARKHAM, ONTARIO L3R 0E3
Questions/Comments?
Please call 1-800-268-6232 from
9am to 4pm EST weekdays

I've always told my mother she should write a cookbook titled *Cooking for Ingrates*. In the face of much offspring hostility, she brought into the house such wonders as caraway seeds, mushrooms, hot mustard, and cheeses other than cheddar. And we all remember the great excitement that afternoon when she came in the back door carrying a wok. My mother is shown here wearing the dress she wore in Montreal for Expo '67.

Moose

One evening during art school in 1982, I was at a friend's place when the phone rang—it was Allison from the floor above, inviting us all up for a spaghetti dinner. Free food? *We're in.* So we went upstairs, where I ate three portions before Allison said, "Oh, by the way, it's made from ground moose meat." Okay—I was tempted to puke, but at the same time, the spaghetti *was* really delicious, so I had to be honest with myself. Thus, my decision was to neither puke nor to eat any more servings. Stalemate.

This sort of situation has been following me my whole life. Growing up, I'd get a distant early warning from my mother, saying that "Tonight we're having pheasant for dinner." Were I a Rothschild, this would be good news. In *my* family, pheasant meant having to be careful not to swallow any lead shot and wondering why it is that pheasant, prairie chicken and grouse seem to be birds entirely devoid of white meat.

Whenever you see a Canadian historical photo, there is an almost scientific certainty that there is a moose within rifleshot of the camera's lens, even in photographs taken in cities. The moose, possibly more than the beaver, is an animal whose gait and size and personality lives within the quiet nooks of the national imagination, chewing away at a blueberry bush while small birds tickle its antlers. Moose are also interesting because, of the undomesticated larger Canadian land mammals, they're the ones who seem closest to being on the brink of forming meaningful bonds with humans. Under most circumstances, they're peaceful and good-natured, but you *do* have to watch out for mating season and all that pesky rutting. Canada, unsurprisingly, abounds with tales of tamed moose charming a community—and being named Bruce in the process.

Mary Maxim

GRAPH-STYLE

KNITTING PATTERN

No. 4022
MEN'S CARDIGAN
RAGLAN or
SET-IN SLEEVES
SIZES: 38-40-42-44

Bulky Weight

FOR GUARANTEED RESULTS USE ONLY MARY MAXIM BRANDED YARNS

Oirland

My great aunt on my mother's side, Aunt Constance, was a never-married high-school gym teacher from Regina. She was born Constance Campbell in 1903. We'll never know what her interior life was truly like—whether she loved and lost or, well, *anything*—she left few traces of her time on earth, and those that survive indicate a saddish, unreflective existence. And while it's bad manners to speak ill of the dead, it can be said, with much humility, that she was cranky, a bit boring and slightly prudish. So, imagine the glee which my Aunt Mary Jane Campbell, born 1941, must have felt as she was sent to tour Europe with Aunt Con in the summer of 1961. Few tortures could be more sublime than this.

So, there they were, "Miss & Match," their Baedeker guides in hand, Mary Jane seeking romance and dreaminess in a Venetian gondola, Aunt Con seeking a firm mattress and breakfasts containing bacon and eggs cooked under sanitary conditions. Events climaxed in Edinburgh, where Mary Jane, thrilled at gaining contact with the Campbell family's Scottish roots, was bubbling over in a bus that was groaning up the hill to Holyrood Castle, when Aunt Con finally snapped. "For God's sake, Mary Jane, what's this fuss all about? Your father was never Scottish. He's as Irish as rotten potatoes. He only pretended to be Scottish because the Irish couldn't get jobs during the Depression. That's why he was always hamming up the Scottish nonsense."

"What? But what about you and Mom?"

"We're genuine Scots, but nobody cares about a woman's history."

Good times ahoy.

Several decades later, but before Mary Jane told me this story, I spent a month in Sligo, Ireland, doing research for a book I never wrote, and everyone there kept asking me how many Irish relatives I had. It would have been such fun to ham up the "Oirish" side of my roots, had I known they existed.

A few years before that, in a magazine piece I wrote in 1987, one of my first, I used the phrase "paddy wagon." My editor crossed this out with red wax pencil, and I had no idea why. I fought to keep it in, because I could see no reason why "paddy" might be offensive. I mean, how corny: *Those Irish are all drunks and need a special vehicle to haul them to the clink every night.* Have we learned nothing from the Kennedys?

This isn't about kilts versus leprechauns; it's about assimilation and how the notion of normality evolves over time. The U.S. has a melting pot culture. Canada's isn't quite a melting pot, but no one's really sure what it is … a quilt? … a salad? … a sandwich? … a soup? … a piñata? … a mosaic? What we know for sure is that what was once alien becomes Canadian in the end, and that in the future our country may well quite cheerfully resemble the outer-space cocktail-lounge scenes from *Star Wars.*

Oka is two things to Canadians …

1) A small town in Quebec where, since 1893, nearby Trappist monks have been making a beloved semi-soft surface-ripened cheese.

2) A Canadian shorthand for the complex, ongoing, painful and often surrealistic coexistence between First Nations people and everybody else. In 1990, the Oka town council planned to convert a nine-hole golf course into an eighteen-hole golf course on top of, among other things, a Mohawk graveyard! What they were thinking? Who knows. This one decision triggered off ultra-violent confrontations between police forces, the Canadian Armed Forces, Indian tribes across North America, and just about everybody else except the Trappist monks.

Above: Members of the Cold Lake First Nations, in a show of solidarity with the struggles at Oka, set fire to a wooden trestle train bridge that leads to the Canadian Forces Base at Cold Lake, Alberta..

Plywood

Let me warn you: I am about to be very bitter for the next few paragraphs.

Okay, here goes. Most people can't remember a life without plywood, but plywood for the masses is a recent phenomenon that really kicked into full gear after WWII. How did people ever manage to build rumpus rooms or tree forts before then?

Plywood is beautiful. Flat! Woody looking! Little eye-shaped slots where the knots were! I love the stuff. It's clean and smart and can be used to make just about anything. Bonus: it smells like, well, *plywood*—which in turn smells of growing up in the suburbs and of new houses being built. Plywood smells best of all when mingled with the aroma of freshly poured concrete. Now there's a fragrance opportunity just waiting for someone to put in a bottle: *"Subdivision—the scent."*

But, of course, the trouble with Canada is that plywood, along with newsprint, is about *all* we make with our wood. Our good stuff gets sent away, 2003 being a record year for raw log exports—and then after we've waved good-bye to it, we sit and mope about joblessness. Argh! This is actually my biggest problem with Canadian industry. We give our stuff away for peanuts, then whine about no jobs in the unemployment lineup … something's wrong. There are only so many people who can get jobs answering 1-800 phone numbers for Microsoft or the J. Crew catalogue. Pretty soon we'll have this spooky pretend economy, where all anyone does is make phone calls or answer them. It's really stupid. Even stupider is that in all of B.C., the country's third-biggest plywood exporting province, there's *not one plywood-moulding machine.*

My frustration with this issue is a theme whenever I get going about Canada. I can see this is going to be my official rant in the old folks' home. I'm going to be very crusty and bitter, so for everybody's sake I hope we've rectified the problem by then.

S BURD

OHN PACKOWSKI

R

Reach for the Top

If Canada has given nothing else to the world, it is game show hosts and TV news anchors, some of whom got their start hosting *Reach for the Top*.

Reach for the Top started in 1961 in Vancouver. It was a Canada-wide quiz show in which your high school's four (theoretically) smartest students got to go on TV to battle with the brainiacs of other schools. Invariably, your school never won—or even made it to the finals. Hence, your school's quartet of brilliance inevitably brought a deep stain of shame on your school. Well, not really.

Getting on *Reach for the Top* wasn't necessarily a task that was given to a school's smartest students. Usually, it went to the students who really *really* wanted to be on the show, I.Q. be damned. Technically, all students had to be notified that they could apply as contestants, but this tended to be a faintly photocopied notice that appeared on the nurse's office bulletin board for three hours before it mysteriously vanished.

The show continues to this day in a form somewhat altered from the original, and, if I'm brutally honest (I can't believe I'm writing this), it's actually kind of fun to watch your school get trashed by another school. I have no idea why.

Royal Conservatory

It's a rare Canadian musician who can't open up their piano bench or violin case or old trunk to reveal a dozen music books bearing the Royal Conservatory of Music's imprimatur. Perhaps my old grade six music book on the right triggered a memory of your own Royal Conservatory books. The conservatory is a Canadian-only secret society that exists among musicians. My own secret password? The first eight bars of "Sarabande in D Minor."

Sadly, I didn't pay too much attention to my Royal Conservatory lessons, and as a result, I play mechanically, lazily and with a flawed ear. I'm able to tell, at most, the difference between major and minor chords. As decades pass, it now takes four to five weeks to get my fingers back into playing shape, which is to say, to be able to play badly. Piano playing is like typing— you either learn to do it properly at an early age, or you're forever relegated to being a two-fingered typist (as I am).

My piano teacher was the gifted Mrs. Solnes, who for years endured the results of my lazy technique, nonexistent practice habits and pig-ignorant comprehension of why musical theory is important. *Mrs. Solnes, I owe you a wicker duck full of soap for your patience and diplomatic finesse. But why didn't you just phone my parents and tell them to have me pack it in?*

ROYAL
CONSERVATORY OF MUSIC

VI

University of Toronto

Price $1.25

GRADE VI
PIANOFORTE
EXAMINATION

THE FREDERICK HARRIS MUSIC CO. LIMITED/OAKVILLE, ONTARIO, CANADA

Printed in Canada

Scary Bank Calendar

Growing up, every time I had to go with my parents into a Royal Bank, there on the wall I saw this big evil dark blue calendar with gold numbers. What I always believed about these numbers is that they weren't telling you the date—they were actually telling you how many more days you had left … *until you die*. I don't know what the bank was thinking. Did they pay fear consultants to design these things?

BANQUE ROYALE

JUIN

24

Shocked & Appalled

Canada's one true national art form is the indignant letter to the editor. Canadians *love* being shocked and appalled in print and take great care that their indignation is cutting yet subtle, with a hint of passive aggression. Sample: *"It's not so much that I'm shocked and appalled— I'm simply ... disappointed. I expected better from you. That's okay. It's only my opinion."* Ouch!

This almost universal editorial-page need to make disapproving clucks seems at odds with our national predilection for tolerance, but not really. Canadians tend to deal with problems either by signing petitions or by forming committees to investigate issues—thus ensuring that nothing ever happens abruptly, and Canada remains peaceful and static. Letters to the editor serve a valid function. If a petition or a committee is unavailable, letters pick up the emotional slack, guaranteeing that everything ends *sans* hubbub.

S M L XL XXL

P M G TG TTG

St. Pierre et Miquelon

Any child in North America knows the thrill of driving down the highway looking for licence plates from as many states and provinces as possible. Arizona! *Yawn*. New Mexico! *Not quite as big of a yawn.* A plate from the real Mexico—*pretty cool.* Hawaii! *Okay, that's pretty cool, too*—but in B.C., not as hard to find as you might think.

Among licence plate collectors—a variant of what the Brits affectionately call "train spotters"—there remains the Holy Grail of plate scouting. No, it's not Puerto Rico (rare, mind you), nor is it Rhode Island (oh please), but, rather, SPM—St. Pierre et Miquelon—two itty-bitty islands a one-hour ferry ride south of Newfoundland, attached to each other by a skinny isthmus that almost vanishes during high tide. These islands are technically, legally, weirdly, astonishingly, part of France. Yes, that's correct, *France.* To be on these islands is as French as being in downtown Paris.

St. Pierre et Miquelon are like other tiny places in that a disproportionate amount of their GDP comes from the sale of postage stamps to teenage boys worldwide. Many Canadians, mostly guys, briefly bond with St. Pierre et Miquelon during their adolescent stamp-collecting phase. Because the place is so tiny (population 6,996), few letters get mailed from there. Throw e-mail into the mix, and mail stops almost altogether.

As a teenager, I occasionally had a job fantasy where I lived in a lighthouse at one end of the islands, smoked Gitanes, scowled, chewed baguettes and mailed letters with St. Pierre postmarks to a dummy address in Toronto. I'd then sell these genuinely "mailed" letters at vastly inflated prices—certainly enough to allow me to continue my lighthouse existence.

A friend of mine admitted that she dreams of shedding her sedate Canadian life by scurrying off and dating one of St. Pierre et Miquelon's beret-topped civil servants. "But it's never going to happen," she says. "For starters, it's too hard, too boring and too expensive to actually get to the place, and once you've seen your third gift shop, well, I guess the dream would fade, and I need this little daydream to get through my days."

Tiens!

Adieu! Farewell, our small island friends! We shall miss you!

Left and above: Edward Burtynsky, *Nickel Tailings #34 & #35,* Sudbury, Ontario, 1996

GREAT LAKES REGION

TORONTO AREA

EMPLOYEES' OPERATING TIMETABLE

74

TAKING EFFECT AT 0001 SUNDAY, OCTOBER 26th, 1969

ALL TIMES SHOWN ARE EASTERN STANDARD

WORK SAFELY — NO INVESTMENT PAYS BETTER DIVIDENDS

S. E. SPENCER
MANAGER
TORONTO

R. G. MESSENGER
OPERATIONS MANAGER
TORONTO

R. W. BOWMAN
SUPT. TRANSPORTATION
TORONTO

Sudbury

My grandmother, Jean Elizabeth Young, was the first woman in Sudbury ever to get a licence to drive a car. It takes so little to create a family mythology.

In the early 1920s, Jean Elizabeth met my grandfather, Douglas Charles Wilkin Coupland. DCW came from a family of horse breeders in Saint Mary's, Ontario, and was in Sudbury working as an exodontist treating Canadian Pacific Railroad employees. He was a quiet soul to begin with, and, on top of this, he was desperately lonely and miserable, dumping his daily bucket of bloody teeth into the nickel slag while contemplating spending the evening in a lonely bed-sit room. His life must have been quite charmless until he saw Jean Elizabeth in her car, rambling over the lifeless asteroid of acidic scorched earth of Sudbury in the 1920s. They were married, whereupon she put down her foot, said, "We're out of here, buster. We're going to go to Ottawa, and we are going to be successful." And so off they went.

But they left behind them a place where a portion of our family's soul still rests.

Fortunately for Sudburians, a billion years ago, a meteorite slammed into the planet at the spot where Sudbury now rests. Rock to the south of the crater was pushed north, making the impact crater oval shaped and creating earth's richest nickel deposit.

Then came the 1950s and the Cold War, and with it, the U.S. government's need to stock up on "non-communist nickel." (What a great phrase.)

By the 1960s, Sudbury was so ravaged by smelting emissions that NASA used the local landscape as a lunar testing ground for astronauts. In 1972 came the Superstack, which releases emissions high up into the jet stream, doing God only knows what to the planet—but, since then, plants have been growing in Sudbury.

CALGARY Exhibition & STAMPEDE

$2.00

OFFICIAL SOUVENIR PROGRAM & PHOTO ALBUM

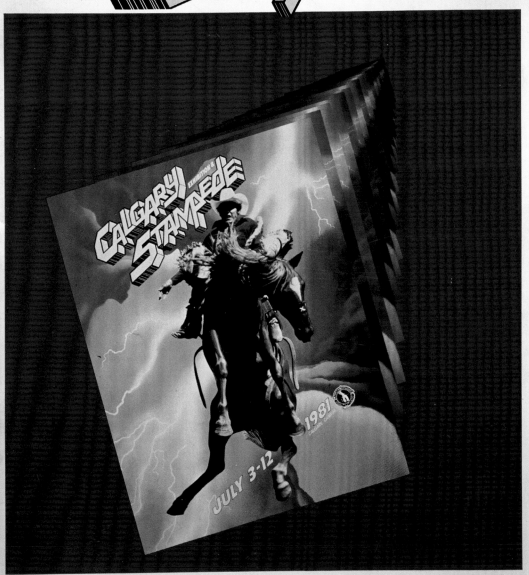

JULY 3-12   1981

Massey-Ferguson
MF 165 Tractor

Advanced Ferguson System/gasoline-diesel/wide row-crop or standard clearance models

Terry Fox

In my writings on Canada, I've deliberately kept names and personalities as far from the surface as possible. In Canada, the moment you mention a name—any name—you begin to divide its citizens. We're a very cranky lot that way. The only exception I can think of is Terry Fox. Canadians agree that he is a true hero. Terry is the only citizen who can never divide us. In the words of one of Canada's best-known reporters, "He gave us a dream as big as our country."

Terry was born in Winnipeg on July 28, 1958. In 1977, at eighteen, he and his family were living in B.C., when he was diagnosed with bone cancer—his right leg had to be removed 15 centimetres (6 inches) above the knee. After this experience, Terry decided to do what he could to find a cure for cancer. He decided to run across Canada, attempting to run the equivalent of one marathon a day, to raise money for and awareness of cancer research. Hang on a second— running a marathon *every day* for *months*? Yes. You read that correctly.

Terry called his journey the Marathon of Hope. It began on April 12, 1980, in St. John's, Newfoundland. There, Terry dipped his prosthetic leg into the Atlantic Ocean, hoping that, at the marathon's end, he would dip it into the Pacific in Vancouver. Terry then ran an average of 42 kilometres (26 miles!) every day for 143 days, but on Monday, September 1, he ran his last stretch. The cancer had spread to his lungs. It stopped his mission just east of Thunder Bay, Ontario.

Terry died in June of 1981 at the age of twenty-two. Canada's population at that time was 24.82 million people, and Terry's wish to raise one dollar for every citizen had by then been realized. Almost twenty-five years later, it's not implausible to say that over a billion dollars will one day be raised for cancer research because of Terry. He is, by all measures, immortal.

Wait.

I have to pause for a second here.

I mean …

At the very least, Terry's story can only make any of us wonder about what's true and what's junk—it makes us reprioritize our inner lives.

Terry Fox had a special attachment to this sock. He wore it continuously on his prosthesis from the day he left home on April 7, 1980, to begin his Marathon of Hope. Terry became so attached to it that he continued to wear it for about three months after the run ended.

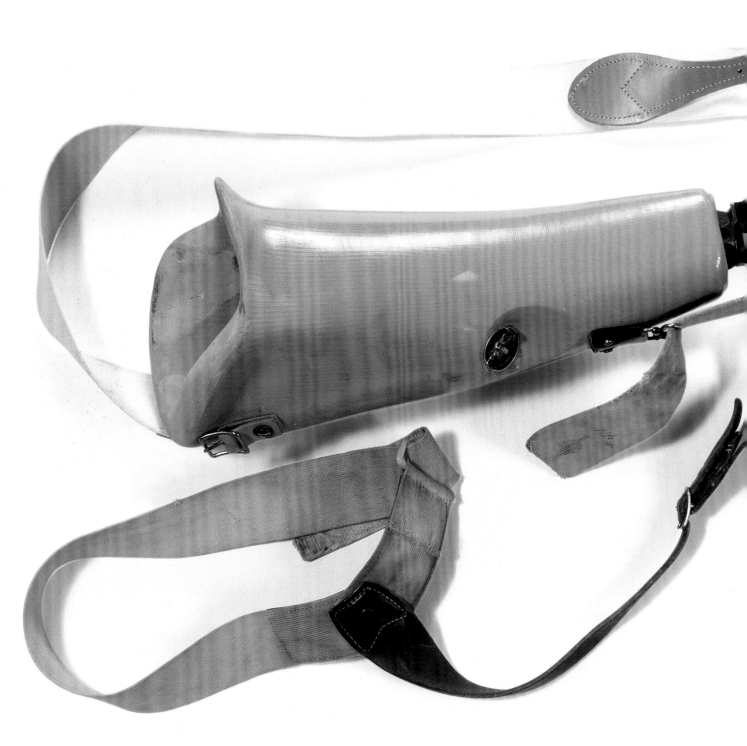

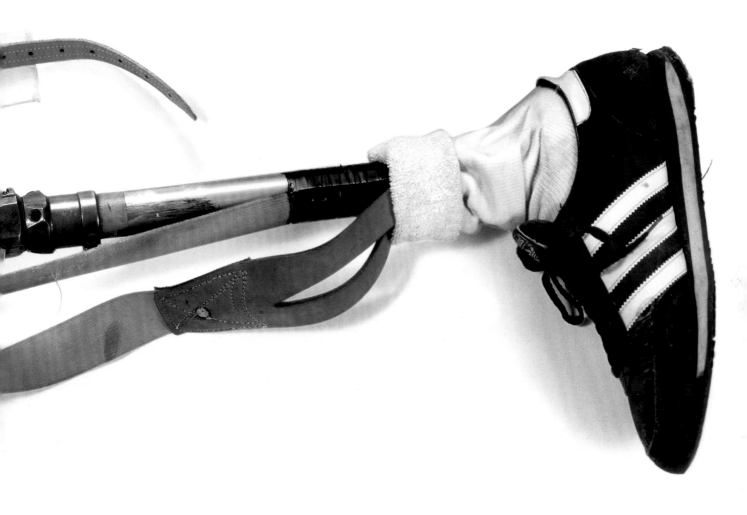

In the fall of 2002, I drove to the Terry Fox Public Library in Port Coquitlam, B.C., where Terry Fox's prosthetic leg, his running shoe and his sock, all from the Marathon of Hope, are kept in a Plexiglas display case. Inside the library, I was allowed to take Terry's prosthetic leg, still clad in an Adidas runner, and photograph it in an activity room against a white seamless paper backdrop. The surroundings of the photo shoot were humble—folded-up tables, stacks of chairs and a polished beige floor.

The artificial leg looks harsh and mechanical, but with prostheses, you need to go beyond looks and focus on what works and what doesn't. This leg got Terry halfway across Canada. A second leg was used as a spare when this one broke down, something that rarely happened. The leg is an efficient combination of springs, gears and fibreglass. There is a valve that released pressure around the stump of Terry's leg. The keys were used to adjust the tension in the springs.

The shoe is one of several pairs Terry wore during the Marathon of Hope. The shoe on his natural leg took most of the wear, so though he changed the shoe on his natural leg eight times, the shoe on his prosthetic foot required no changing. The underside of the shoe on Terry's prosthetic leg is covered in what looks like soggy cornflakes, but is, in fact, decomposed squeeze-on goo used to extend the lives of running shoes.

A summer afternoon swim, Jackfish Lake, Ontario. Terry wore this particular kind of grey shorts during his marathon because they were the only ones that bore no logo.

Previous pages: Ken Steacy, *Toronto, 2504 A.D.*

Above: Posters on a hoarding at Queen Street and Spadina Avenue, Toronto, Halloween 2003

Toronto

Toronto was once the city that Canadians loved to ~~hate~~ dislike. Why? Simple. One day, as happened with Microsoft, the numbers came in, and Toronto was suddenly the biggest dog on the block. I remember the year it happened, sometime in the mid-1970s, when Toronto's population eclipsed that of Montreal. I was with my uncle and we were driving south from the Gatineau Mountains into Toronto. Somewhere on the 401, we saw the highway sign with the new population numbers—white letters on green. It felt like a real moment, and it was.

Most of the nation's commerce and culture is regulated and multiplied within Toronto's grid. In a book, I once described Toronto as "the Yellow Pages sprung to life in three dimensions, peppered with trees and veined with ice water," and I think that definition still, to some degree, sticks—in a good way. When you factor in its suburbs and what social scientists call its "conurbation," Toronto is a massive economy unto itself, larger than that of most of the world's nations. You simply can't deny its power. Human hearts are jealous; Toronto was an easy target, up until 2003.

In 2003, Toronto was blindsided by the SARS virus, a sci-fi plague both from hell and the distant and awful future. A few months later, after limping through the wreckage of its economy, the city melted down during a catastrophic power failure. The year 2003 was an awful time for its citizens, and for the first time in its history, the hearts of Canadians went out to Torontonians and have largely stayed with them since. Toronto has been humanized and, because of its vulnerability, at long last has won a form of affection.

Alternate way of pronouncing Toronto? *Tranna.*

HEALTH ALERT NOTICE

SEVERE ACUTE RESPIRATORY SYNDROME (SARS)

HEALTH CANADA MESSAGE FOR INTERNATIONAL TRAVELLERS
ARRIVING IN OR RETURNING TO CANADA

To the traveller:

During your time outside Canada, you may have travelled to a SARS-affected area.

On the plane:

If you are currently on an airplane and have a fever **AND** one or more of the following respiratory symptoms – cough, shortness of breath or difficulty breathing – Health Canada recommends that you notify one of the airline flight crew immediately.

Off the plane:

You should monitor your health for 10 days. If you develop a fever **AND** one or more of the following symptoms during a 10-day period – chills, muscle aches, feeling generally "unwell", headache, cough, shortness of breath or difficulty breathing – Health Canada recommends that you seek medical advice as soon as possible. Call ahead to your physician or your local public health unit/department for information about the appropriate Emergency Department or established SARS Centre you should visit for medical assessment. While not all travellers with these symptoms have developed SARS, it is nevertheless important to ensure that if you do get these symptoms, you stay away from other people until you have been assessed for SARS. These actions are very important for stopping the spread of SARS.

You can obtain up-to-date health alert information from Health Canada about the situation at **www.sars.gc.ca**. In Canada, you can call **1-800-454-8302**.

Self-assessment questionnaire:
(1 questionnaire per family)

Please <u>circle</u> YES or NO to the following questions:

1. Do you have a fever?   YES   NO

2. Do you have one or more of the
   following symptoms:
   cough, shortness of breath **OR**
   difficulty breathing?   YES   NO

3. Have you been in contact with a
   SARS-affected person in the last
   10 days?   YES   NO

This Health Alert Notice will be given back to you by the Custom's Agent. Please save it for 10 days.

Version 3A
Date: May 16th, 2003

Canada

Treeplanters

The world has many wretched jobs awaiting the young, the idealistic and the gullible. In Canada, one of those jobs is called treeplanting. Typically, it's thirty-one days of not bathing, crapping off the end of logs and swatting blackflies the size of olives. During merciful forays into Prince George or Nippigon motels, you enter blood brawls over who gets the first shower, and hence all the hot water. Afterwards, the locals beat you up in the parking lots of pubs, screaming, *"Tree hugger!"* Quick question: if you're not a tree hugger, then you're a what— a *tree hater?*

Before the airlines in Canada melted down, there was one called Canada 3000. I called it Treeplanter Airlines, because every time I looked at the gates before boarding, the waiting passengers seemed to entirely consist of fuzzy-cheeked Ontario boys and rosy-cheeked Quebec girls out for a summer of sunburns, repetitive stress disorders and disillusionment with mankind.

Eliza Massey, *A swampy day for Steve,* 1991 (left) and *Cindy in a burn,* 1991 (above)

Eliza Massey, *Megan having a break*, 1991

Eliza Massey, *Sandy mentally preparing herself for another run*, 1992

The 16th Canadian Machine Gun Company fighting amid shell craters. Battle of Passchendaele, Belgium, November 1917. There were 15,564 casualties over the 8-kilometre (5-mile) advance.

War

The GDP of Canada is about equal to the combined GDPs of Michigan, Indiana and Illinois. Imagine if you went to the governors of these three states and said, "Oh, by the way, the three of you must give military protection and economic nutrition to every square metre of land up to, and possibly including, the North Pole." You'd be laughed out of the room. But that's exactly what Canada has to do. Do we have a huge fleet of high-tech warships and jet aircraft? No. We have dick all. It's depressing. I grew up in a military family and believe in being prepared. I've also lived in countries all over the world, and Canada is the only one where you can go for months and months and never once see any evidence of the armed forces. It's not because they're well concealed—I think it's because they don't much exist. An hour ago, on the highway in Vancouver, I saw an olive-green truck with funny-coloured plates, and nobody in the car could tell if it was a military vehicle or a movie prop. Sometimes, Canada's sense of itself reminds me of the trilogy of Hobbit movies, in which Frodo keeps the most important object in the entire universe stuck inside the pocket of some shabby trousers or on a string around his neck. *For God's sake, you morons—take better care of the ring! The ring is Canada!*

Does Canada piggyback on the U.S. military? Yes—and no. Pretend that the U.S. also includes Canada. Even if that were the case, the distribution of technology and troops still wouldn't be much different than it is today. The Goose Bay NORAD base would still be at Goose Bay. Submarine bases on the lower forty-eight states might be a little bit more to the north, but then maybe not. Nobody's going to invade Canada through Hudson Bay. Alaska flanks much of the North, and Greenland keeps the English from attacking Nova Scotia. As well, Canada's not stupid, and all across the country, any number of its monitoring systems and programs run in tandem with those of the U.S. Our national military policy is based both on a mix of geographical luck and chronic underfunding—after all, who's going to pay the tab—Michigan and Indiana and Illinois?

As a way of acknowledging the cozy location of its real estate and its financial inability to protect what is the world's second-largest country, Canada's policy since WWII has been one of peacekeeping. That sounds like sucky wishful thinking, but, at the same time, it's a realistic decision once you inspect the cards we've been dealt. This decision is also a *real decision,* based on the facts—I've said it before, and I'll say it here—Canada is not an imperialist nation. We're not out for more land. We can only ever have what we have now. This keeps us humble and forever on guard.

What about wars not on our own turf? Americans love their country, and if it goes to war, they'll support it. It's their country and their choice, so good on them. When they ask us, "Why aren't you joining our war?" and we say, *"We love our country, too, and we're supporting our own country in the way it has chosen to act,"* Americans get angry. Americans like to treat Canada as either a nation or a fifty-first state, depending on what suits their needs at the moment. But being a nation means you have sovereignty and the freedom to choose your way. You just can't use mere political longing to turn Canada into a fifty-first state.

One other thing to remember is that Canada's military is depressingly underfunded. Even if we wanted to send out our troops tomorrow, it might be a moot decision, which is almost a bit embarrassing. Most Canadians are aware of the chronic military underfunding. Suddenly, we're back to where we began, with the realization that we have the budget of a middle-American tri-state region. What brave politician is going to take money from other programs to fund the military?

If you take the long view—which the American government always does and which the Canadian government (unfortunately) almost never does—you realize that wars come and go, and sometimes, like WWI and WWII, Canadians were in the trenches years and years before the Americans, and other times, as in Vietnam, Canada said "Thanks but no thanks." When WW3 arises, Canada may be in there with the plasma beams years ahead of the Americans. It all evens out.

Canadians also know darn well that, more often than not, our existence suits the Americans. We're indeed their back door, their underground railroad, their matrix—or whatever metaphor you choose. In some ways, if the war of 1812 had gone differently and North America was one big United States, the Americans would have had to invent Canada as a diplomatic construct, precisely for all the alternative strategies and options our presence affords them.

Above: Greg Locke, *Hibernia Oil Rig*, 1999

Hibernia is a $5.8-billion structure resting 315 kilometres (200 miles) from the coast of St. John's, Newfoundland, and 320 kilometres from the location of the *Titanic*. It houses a crew of 185 and is designed to withstand icebergs. In one minute, it can extract 110 barrels of oil from beneath the ocean floor.

Left: Nigel Reeves, *Getaway No. 2*, 2003

Who Do You Think You Are?

If Canada has a national motto, it's not *A mari usque ad mare* (from sea to sea) but, rather, *Who do you think you are?* Canadians largely perceive themselves as middle class. Canadians love the middle, not just because it's safe but also because it's inherently democratic and fair. *But* … if you become too different from the others, little bells collectively go ding-ding-ding, and you will be shunned and mocked. Your only option at this point is to leave the country. Should you succeed outside the borders, that's okay, but the second you cross back inside the border, you have to be average again. After all, *who do you think you are?* An indicator of Canada's fondness for the middle is that it has no indigenous luxury brands. There are some luxury items that originate here such as diamonds, pot and gold, but they're not luxury brands.

Not just our laws but also our whole social contract is founded on this assumption about the middle—from it we also have, as an example, a collective knowledge that smoking is a glamourized medical nightmare and that it needs to be treated as nothing less. Roughly a quarter of Canadians smoke, but there can't be one smoker out there who's delusional enough to not know the precise medical disasters it creates for them. I quit smoking on Halloween 1988, and I could start tomorrow, but if I'm honest, it's only our government's unflinching policy of putting photos of diseased body parts on all cigarette packaging that keeps me from lapsing.

Y??

All airports worldwide are known by their three-letter "location identifier" codes. Through an agreed-upon convention, Canadian airport codes start with the letter "Y." This sounds like a boring or bad deal at first, but in the alphabet-soup netherworld of airline codes, when staff in any airport see a "Y," presto, your luggage goes on the correct Canada-bound conveyor belt. Europe also uses a four-letter coding system that makes our "Y" seem even more attractive. Copenhagen is not only CPH but EKCH, too. Palermo is both PMO and LICJ. Moscow is DME and UUDD. Give me YVR or YYZ any day of the week.

Deadheading from Toronto to summer excursion service out of Ottawa, the Ontario Rail Association's ex-CP D10h 4-6-0 1057 and four heavyweight coaches cross CP's Rideau River bridge at Merrickville, Ontario, June 29, 1975.

Bridgewater-bound CN RS18s 1777 and 1781 (re-trucked with A1As from RSC13s) slip through Martin's River, Nova Scotia, with No. 501, September 29, 1980.

THE CANADIAN LOOK

A CENTURY OF SIGHTS AND STYLES / KEN LEFOLII

marijuana grow ops

A growing hazard

BChydro

What is a grow op?

A marijuana growing operation, or grow op, is an illegal enterprise in which marijuana plants are raised to maturity and then sold for a profit. To maintain optimal growing conditions, grow ops are mostly set up indoors, in urban residences and industrial rental properties, although some are on rural properties.

Local criminal elements as well as organized crime are involved in marijuana production. Much of the product is exported from B.C. to other provinces and the U.S.

Grow ops affect everyone from neighbours to landlords to emergency responders and impose a cost burden on all of us. The number of grow ops in B.C. is on the rise, increasing the risks to the community.

Accidents waiting to happen

A house in which a grow op is operated may use three to 10 times the power of an average home. Bypasses, done to conceal the high electricity usage, are often done by people with little knowledge of electrical wiring. The type of wiring modification shown here is all too common in marijuana

growing operations, set up in properties rented from (usually) unsuspecting landlords in residential neighbourhoods. The risk of fire is just one of many hazards that threaten the safety of communities and cost property owners a significant amount each year.

Indoor grow-ops are an entrenched way of cash-crop farming in Vancouver and much of the rest of Canada. The telltale signs of a grow-op are unmowed lawns, humidity in the windows and one (and only one) light that never gets turned off, as two bulbs would use up too much electricity. Growers like to rent spacious houses with basements, built between 1950 and 1985. They surround my parents' house. I took my mother on a grow-op tour of the neighbourhood one afternoon. She thought it was quite funny, "And it helps explain why we never get trick-or-treaters at the door any more."

Yanks

Pot is both a big deal and not a big deal in Canada. On the one hand, it's Canada's largest industry. On the other hand, it's cheap and it's good, but do people quit their jobs, buy cotton drawstring pants, tie-dyed shirts and bongs and move into basement suites to devote their lives to it? No. That's not what people do when given an overabundance of pot. There'll always be potheads, but then there'll always be cheerleaders and nerds. It's like a statistical given. How many unemployed potheads do I know now? None. Have I ever known any? Sure. What happened to them? They grew up and got lives. That's how it works.

The reason I mention all of this is to point out that people from other countries come to Canada and see pot being treated casually yet with reasonableness. The sight of this forces visitors to question the value of pot laws in their own countries. There's no right or wrong here, but there are practical issues to consider. When you think about pot in Canada, you should also look at other aspects of the culture that are demonized by outsiders—universal medical care springs to mind—and then ask yourself, "Hey—why isn't Canada an overmedicated and shady sleaze pit?"

This past summer, I met a woman in Alaska whose mother had Alzheimer's. Her parents had to get divorced and her mother had to be declared bankrupt, before she could receive even the smallest portion of medical care. This didn't totally shock me, but the next day, in Seattle, I met a woman whose mother and father had to do the exact same thing. Could this have happened in Canada? No.

I have scores of good American friends, and every one of them has, at some point, accepted a crap job solely for the medical coverage, throwing away the most important years of their lives. At the same time, I have yet to meet a single person in Canada who's taken a job simply for the medical coverage. Not one. Ever. That's a vital and astonishing thing to consider. Americans can always point out Canadians in Canada waiting in line for a cardiac procedure, yet all you need is Google to locate forty-four million Americans with no medical insurance whatsoever. *Forty-four million.*

Some Americans have trouble with Canada because we're a living case study of how the centre can hold when exposed to evils. Our politicians are being urged by outside forces to harmonize our penal laws with theirs, not because our laws are inherently bad but merely because if we don't, it might make the laws of other countries ripe for questioning. That's no reason to change a policy, in Canada or anywhere else.

Here's something else: around the year 2000, Canadians stopped identifying themselves as a place that existed only as an alternative to U.S. culture. Canada is almost a hundred years younger than the U.S., so it comes as no surprise that it took Canada longer to get a fuller sense of itself. We like universal health care. We like the freedom to be genuinely different (instead of just a little bit different) from others. We know how to handle our drugs and guns. We like nature, and we want it to remain nature. We don't clog our courts with nonsense lawsuits.

Europeans have been quite stunned to see that in recent years Canada and the U.S. have had conflicting national values. It used to be almost a given that Canada was a big bland twin of Minnesota, stitched onto the U.S. like a bungled organ transplant. While it's foolish and naïve to ignore how much we have in common with the U.S.—in all honesty, it's an astonishing friendship—it's equally foolish to have this commonality lull us into morphing into a U.S. clone. Sometimes, Canadians seem knee-jerkishly anti-American, and yes, this can sometimes be very *very* annoying. Usually, it's just huffing and puffing, but it's also vital in order for Canada to remain Canadian.

Here's a thought: Canada's economy is a bit bigger than that of Texas. Texans are good citizens and love their country, but they must sometimes wonder what would have happened if history had played out differently and their state had remained a sovereign nation.

Depending on when and where you grew up in Canada, your view of Americans can swing many ways. My experience from kindergarten to twelfth grade was, "Just shut up, because by 2000 we're going to be the fifty-first state. It's an inevitability, okay?" Who was saying this? Teachers. The papers. And in the 1980s and early 1990s, it was a recurring conversational theme with most Canadians. Canada has never felt more in bed with the U.S. than it did around 1990. It felt diabolical and bizarre that we had something so great and we were tossing it away. And then came 2000, and—*poof!*—suddenly we're distinct. Was it the Internet? Was it cell phones? Was it satellite TV?

From a global viewpoint, many countries are either becoming smaller and/or stronger, as well as generating a fuller sense of what defines them—not just Canada. I'm thinking of Ireland, Quebec, Spain's Catalan and Basque regions, and the recently reconfigured nations of Balkan Europe and the former Soviet Union. So there's a larger and incontrovertible trend at play here; Canada's no different. At the same time, it can't be denied that the U.S., in its own way, is becoming much more distinctly itself, too.

Canada and the U.S. have never needed a good fence in order to be good neighbours, and they don't need one now. For Canadians who get fed up with Canada, there has always been the option of the U.S., and vice versa. It says wonderful things about the two countries that neither one feels itself being inundated by each other's immigrants. The grass is, to be coy, green on both sides of the fence.

Geoffrey James, *Uplands,* 1999 From the series "A Better Way of Life"

Geoffrey James, *Paradise Canyon,* 1990. From the series "Lethbridge"

Zut!

Bad French is a given in English-speaking Canada. The Canadian government mandates that students learn just enough French to allow them to speak it without joy or competence. It then rewards them with dead-end pseudo-bilingual make-work jobs.

Even though I was a member of the high school French club from 1976 to 1978, my French remains pathetic. The only true linguistic breakthrough I ever made with the language was in 1990-something, when the woman next to me on a flight from London said, "You do know the secret to speaking French well, don't you?"

"Actually, uh, no. What is it?"

"Do you remember the skunk from Warner Bros.' cartoons?"

"Yeah—Pepé Le Pew—the guy who was always falling in love with the black cat who sat on a freshly painted bench and got a white stripe down her back."

"Exactly."

"So then, what's the secret?"

"When you're speaking French, pretend that you're him and speak with a comical exaggerated accent."

"You're mad. You can't be serious."

"Can't I?"

It's so sick and weird, but it *works*. Try it. If I can pull it off, *you* can pull it off.

Zzzzzzzzz ...
... the Sleepy Little Dominion

When I was growing up, the gamekeepers at a nearby golf course would smash the eggs of Canada geese nesting near the water holes. My brother would rescue eggs before they were wrecked, and we incubated them in my father's den in a Johnny Walker box lined with aluminum foil and heated by a 40-watt light bulb. Humidity in the box was maintained by bowls of water placed beside the eggs and by intermittent spritzes of water from an old Windex bottle. The eggs had to be turned over a few times a day, and we were on constant hatching alert, as hatching day was always the best day of the year. When baby Canada geese hop out of their eggs, they're turbocharged little bundles of fluff-packed fun. They're like brilliant children and have an endearing need to seek out warm body crevasses in which to sleep, be they human or belonging to our family's princely black Lab, Ranger.

Goslings are alert, affectionate, trusting, curious, loyal and entertaining—the exact characteristics we also treasure in our human friends. It was pure delight to watch them tumble and peep daily across our lawn, pond, patio and (J-Cloths in hand) kitchen floor. Because of their innocence, everything was permitted.

Goslings, it must be said, also become coltish and decidedly less cute after a few weeks in the world, but this only makes them more endearing as, feather by feather, you watch their white cheek patches take form and their necks elongate by the hour. Their innate curiosity also multiplies during this period, and they want to go everywhere and poke their heads into everything, foraging for adventure as well as stray pellets of duck mash and unraked lawn clippings.

We lived on a cul-de-sac, so cars weren't too much of a worry with the goslings. But as they grew older, that first year we raised them, we did wonder how we were going to teach them to fly. The cul-de-sac was on a mountain slope, and there was no real space for them to practice crash landings. By August, though, there was no denying that the goslings were now geese, and the time had come for them to fledge. As we had no rules to follow, we simply corralled them out on the road at the top of the cul-de-sac and ran down the hill flapping our arms—and they followed us. Sure enough, up they went, landing temporarily on the Williams's roof and then, on from there, flying over other houses and (it still breaks my heart) away from home. They soon landed back on our lawn, but after they'd taken their first flight, you could sense the wildness leaking into their souls. Within a week, they were gone. They didn't forget us—we'd go up the hill to a lake where they found a temporary home, and they responded to our goose calls—and come September, they still landed on the lawn or the roof once or twice. And then winter came, and they were ... gone.

But ...

But then came the next year, early spring. The geese would come home just once. They would land on the roof, always in the morning, and they would honk as if the world depended on it. In robes and T-shirts, we'd run out onto the lawn to look at them there on the roof's apex. Once they'd seen us, there was a brief moment when it wasn't humans and geese, but simply a group of friends happy to be together and alive.

Then off they flew. Just like that. They'd done their duty, and now they vanished into the wild. I've spent my life trying to articulate just what that specific wild was they returned to, for that wild is Canada, and when I think of this country, I think of where the geese go when they leave home.

My family's history in Canada has, on all sides, in all directions, been a non-stop tale of stoic bleakness: insect plagues, savage droughts, endless scrimping, cruel winters, punishing religious Puritanism and soil so rocky it refused to be tilled. Genealogically, there's only so far back we can trace ourselves before we hit the wall—the wall, in my family's case, being Scotland and, to a lesser degree, Ireland. Only my father's grandfather can be successfully traced back to Scotland on paper; on my mother's side, only one great-grandfather, through oral history, can be attached to a small town outside of Balamena in Northern Ireland.

My mother's grandfather—great-grandfather Campbell—grew up on the prairies, and he spent his adult life criss-crossing Canada, family in tow, Bible in hand, spreading the word of God to citizens dying of loneliness, peritonitis, polio, assorted manias and cholera. From High River, Alberta, he took his family to Regina, Winnipeg, Lloydminster, Brandon and numberless smaller stops. Few locales on the planet could have been as hard and barren and mean as the prairies during the first decades of white settlement. They were utterly untamed and still bore the living husks and ghosts of animal species soon to almost vanish.

I think of my grandfather, the impossibly handsome Arthur Lemuel Campbell (of the Irish Campbells), a concrete salesman for Canada Cement, driving his Model-A Ford through the storms and grasshopper clouds and blizzards of Calgary, Saskatoon, Leduc, The Pas and Nowheresville, of his endless hours looking at horizonless lands that promised not just infinite possibilities but infinite nothingness, too. I think of the joy that must have filled his soul when he met his future wife, Jean Campbell, head nurse of a Regina hospital, and of his joy at being transferred to Winnipeg, where he became regional sales director and no longer had to be on the roads that both inspired and spooked him.

The ancestral list goes on—so many of these stoic, sturdy and melancholic forebears—all of them not particularly knowing where they came from, nor where they were headed, guided only by the belief that what came next would be better than what had come before, even during the world wars when the world seemed to deny all logic or humanity. What would these forebears make of the life our family now leads, a life in twenty-first century Vancouver, the least religious jurisdiction in North America, an electronically wired Eden, a city of real-estate flipping, computer games, grow-ops, stock scams, immigration loopholes and iffy nirvana? They'd be disgusted. They'd spit. They'd preach. Or would they? I think that if they could have fast-forwarded into 2004, they'd have done so in a flash. Isn't that what we often crave—to get to the future, faster, sooner, right *now?* We all want to know that what we do in this world creates a jumping off place for future generations.

In 1997, I was in London, England, in Fortnum and Mason's in Piccadilly. I said to the friend I was with, "I hear my mother speaking over there," and I looked, and it wasn't my mother, but rather, it was Carol Shields, a Canadian author, one of my favourites, from Winnipeg, and of my mother's era. It suddenly occurred to me that my mother had a Winnipeg accent—how had I never realized this? The two women even looked alike, and it was such a wonderful feeling, having this unexpected brush with home.

My mother was actually born in London, Ontario, and she spent a lifetime moving from one Canadian locale to another: Winnipeg, Montreal, Kingston, the Canadian Four-Wing Base in Germany, Halifax and Vancouver. She's never lived in a non-Canadian context, nor could I imagine her doing so. She also seems never to have minded pulling up stakes and moving from A to B to C to wherever next. In fact, pulling up stakes is pretty much the norm for most Canadians, moving up, moving west, moving east, but always *moving*. With all of this moving around, I once asked my mother if she ever felt a twinge of anything after my brothers and I left home. She said, "Just the once. It was after Bruce [the youngest] had left, and I was walking up the stairs and looked into his room. It was so empty, and it just hit me like bricks—you were all gone—for good. I burst into tears. Oh, I *knew* you'd all probably be back at one point or other, but it would never be the same. How could it?"

When Canada became a country in 1867, the creation of nations, as we now know them, was still relatively new. For example, the unification of the states that form Italy was still three years away. The U.S. was only eighty-nine years old. Africa, from the perspective of the modern idea of nationhood, was nearly blank.

Because of the relative novelty of nationhood, politicians were left with the need to create a term to describe this new and enormous country that was created in Charlottetown on July 1 of 1867. The term they came up with to describe this new country was "the Dominion of Canada." It was a label that meant Canada represented a place where humans had dominion over creation, a land where the role of citizens would be to care and treasure the bounty they'd been given. It's a poetic term, and technically secular. It's a term that works for just about everybody, and I've yet to hear or read of anybody ever having a quibble with it, let alone wanting to change it.

It is a truth: Canadians *are* blessed. We have yet to become whatever it is we're going to be. We still own our future. Our landscape is bold and fertile and inspires us with its power and its extremes. Whatever may be happening in the rest of the world, the future we build remains bright for us here. What a legacy to inherit, and what did we ever do to deserve this? I've thought about this question, and I don't think it's a matter of what we did to deserve Canada. It's more a matter of asking, what must we do to *continue* deserving it. Our country isn't a prize—it's something we earn every day. Canada isn't something we can take for granted, we have to work at earning it. Forget politicians. Forget much of the claptrap we've been taught. Remember that the *moment* we stop valuing what we have is the moment we will lose it. The land is our blessing and our duty.

I think back to the summer our goslings took flight for the first time. It was late August, in the afternoon, and we'd just had a thunderstorm, which is rare in Vancouver. First there was hail, and then there was rain. The memorable thing is that the rain was warm—almost hot—and I'd never felt warm rain before. Maybe it was the storm and the warm rain that pushed us on, but we'd made the decision that it was now or never, and within the space of a breath, off went our babies.

I think back to my mother and her treks across the land, always in good faith and always with a sense of adventure that she continually underplays. And I can't help thinking of her standing in the middle of the front stairway, holding the newel post, realizing that her own brood has fledged, the tears running down her cheeks.

And then I think back to Terry Fox, crossing the country in that strange summer of 1980, doing the impossible, shocking us as a country with images of what is possible and what isn't. I can't forget his face wrenched with physical pain, and there had to be a tear or two falling down that face, too, mixed in with his sweat. I think of him running onward, always forward, further and further into the heart of this wild majestic country, knowing that however hard the journey might be, he was always heading home.